Starting Ame

The St

Independence Hall

By Edward M. Riley

This 1990 edition is an updated reprint of the original 1954 NPS handbook written by Edward M. Riley. The publication has been a cooperative effort by Eastern National Park & Monument Association and Independence National Historical Park, and is published by Thomas Publications, P.O. Box 3031, Gettysburg, PA 17325.

Printed in the United States of America.

ISBN-0-939631-23-7

Cover illustration: The State House as it appeared about 1776. An engraving by Trenchard based on detail from a painting by Charles Willson Peale as published in the *Columbian Magazine*, c. 1790. Courtesy Independence National Historical Park collection.

Contents

" "THE UNITED STATES was created in Philadelphia on July 4, 1776, when the Continental Congress voted the final form of the Declaration of Independence. The United States was perpetuated on September 17, 1787, when the Federal Convention completed its work on the Constitution and referred it, through Congress, to the individual states for ratification. Both these great decisions were made in the same chamber in what is now called Independence Hall, but was then the Pennsylvania State House. It would still be merely the old State House if independence had not been achieved and if the Constitution had not been ratified and put into effect. The noble building, so venerable to later ages, might not even have survived, but might have been swept away in the surging growth of a modern city. In that case, a few students of history would sometimes remember the site as the stage of those lost causes. Instead, Pennsylvania's State House has become Independence Hall for the entire United States. Nor is that all. On account of the Declaration of Independence, it is a shrine honored wherever the rights of men are honored. On account of the Constitution, it is a shrine cherished wherever the principles of self-government on a federal scale are cherished."—CARL VAN DOREN.

Independence Hall, Photo by Thomas L. Davies.

The Provincial State House

Independence Hall was originally the State House of Pennsylvania. For a half century after the establishment of the Province, the government had no official building. The Assembly, a small legislative body, was compelled to meet in private dwellings rented annually for the purpose or in the old Court House at Second and High (now Market) Streets. In order to meet the needs of the Province, funds were appropriated for the construction of the State House in 1729. At the same time a committee, consisting of Speaker of the Assembly Andrew Hamilton, Assemblyman Dr. John Kearsley, and Councilman Thomas Lawrence, was named to supervise the job. Strong disagreement arose between Hamilton and Kearsley, with each supporting a different location and plan. This disagreement delayed actually beginning work on the building until 1732. In that year the Assembly approved the plan Hamilton advocated and selected the south side of Chestnut Street between Fifth and Sixth Streets as the site. This was then on the outskirts of the city.

The two architectural drawings of the State House which survive are undoubtedly those proposed by Andrew Hamilton, as neither drawing reflects the building as finally built. Hamilton's principal builder, master carpenter Edmund Woolley, was paid for making other drawings of the State House, particularly a set for Governor John Penn to take home to England in 1735, and a set for the tower and steeple additions and other renovations of the 1750's. None of the working drawings survive as they were likely worn out during construction and discarded.

Building the State House was a slow process. The Assembly was not able to meet in the new building until September 1735. Even at that time the walls had not been paneled, nor had all of the window panes been installed. Difficulties of various kinds, especially the scarcity of skilled workmen, kept the building in an unfinished state. Finally, in the summer of 1741, the impatient Assembly ordered that the walls and windows of their chamber be finished at once and the remainder of the building completed without undue delay. Despite this order, plans for completing the Supreme Court Chamber were not submitted until November 1743. The Council Chamber on the upper floor was not ready for occupancy until February 1748. It appears probable that the building was completed about this date.

During construction of the State House the old custom of "raising feasts" was followed. When the main timbers in a building were raised, a sumptuous feast was given for the workmen in celebration of the event. As the building of the State House progressed, there were a number of such feasts, the cost of them borne by the Provincial government.

Shortly after the construction of the State House was started, the Assembly ordered that office buildings be erected as wings to the main building, for the safekeeping of the public papers of the Province. Early in 1736 the wings on each side of the State House were practically completed, but public officials objected strenuously to moving into them. Despite objections, however, it is obvious that the wings were soon occupied by various county and provincial officials. Others also used these small buildings, for in 1739 the Library Company of Philadelphia was granted permission to deposit its books in the upper floor of the west wing. The Library remained there until 1773 when it was moved to Carpenters' Hall. Throughout the Colonial period the doorkeeper of the Assembly and his family also lived in the west wing. Furthermore, during the early years, Indian delegations visiting Philadelphia were sometimes lodged in one of the wings.

These exotic tenants proved a source of worry to the Assembly. Their carelessness with fire posed such a serious threat to public records that, in 1759, the Assembly ordered the erection of a separate building for the use of the Indians. It is thought that one of the two wooden sheds built before the Revolution at the corners of Fifth and Sixth Streets on Chestnut Street was used for this purpose.

Although the 15 years required to build the State House must have been a source of irritation to legislators eager to occupy it, the completed building proved the time was well spent. A most ambitious project for that early date, it emerged a sturdily constructed brick edifice—described at the time as a "large handsome building"—with a facade 107 feet in

Account of Edmund Woolley with Governor John Penn for floor plans and elevation drawings of the State House, 1735-36. Penn Manuscripts, Historical Society of Pennsylvania.

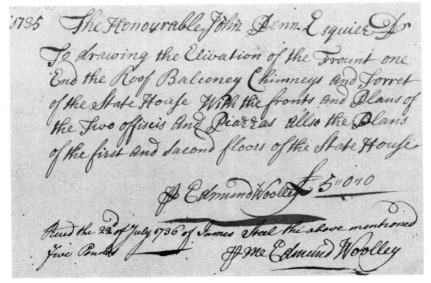

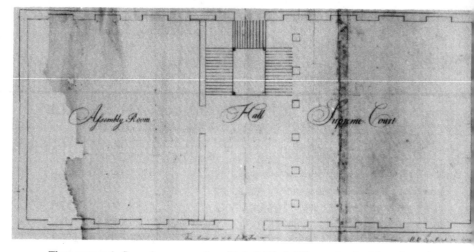

These very early floor plans were not used to build the building as they both have inconsistencies with the way the building was built. The first floor (above) shows the stairway in the south end of the entrance hall, the way it was before the tower was added in the 1750's. In Penn Manuscripts, Warrants and Surveys, Historical Society of Pennsylvania.

length connected by closed arcades, or "piazzas," to wing buildings some 50 feet long. The main building had a decked gambrel roof, balustraded between the chimneys and surmounted by a centrally located cupola. The interior arrangement of the State House provided suitable space for the various agencies of government. The first floor contained two chambers about 40 feet square, separated by a spacious center hall about 20 feet wide. The eastern chamber served as the meeting place of the Assembly. This room, in the words of a contemporary in 1774, was "finished in a neat but not elegant manner." Since the Assembly's sessions were usually secret, the room was provided with a door. The western chamber housed the Supreme Court of the Province and was entered through open archways to provide room for overflowing spectators. The staircase to the upper floor occupied the south end of the central hall. The Provincial Council, the Governor's advisory body, met in a chamber approximately 20 by 40 feet in the southwestern corner of the upper floor. The stair landing separated this room by a small vestibule from a chamber in the southeast corner which was designed as a committee room of the Assembly. The entire Chestnut Street frontage was one room, called the "long gallery," measuring 100 by 20 feet. This long room probably served as a promenade for those waiting to meet the Council, but it was also used for public entertainment and banquets.

It is apparent that the State House was not elegantly furnished. Chairs, tables, curtains, screens, and other items purchased for the building were

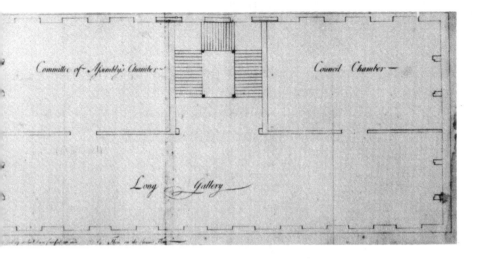

never unduly expensive. However, the silver inkstand, purchased from Philip Syng, of Philadelphia, for the table of the Speaker of the Assembly, and still preserved in Independence Hall, was a most unusual item which cost 25-16-0. The building appears to have been heated originally by open fireplaces for which stoves were later substituted. Lighting was not a serious problem since the meetings rarely continued until darkness; when they did, the Assembly ordered that candles be brought in. There is no known picture of the interior of the State House during the Colonial period; the earliest representation is a painting of the Assembly Room attributed to Edward Savage, "The Congress Voting Independence," which was executed between 1796 and 1817.

In January 1750, shortly after the State House was completed, the Assembly authorized the superintendents of the building to erect a tower to contain a staircase and belfry. Edmund Woolley was entrusted with the construction. By 1753, the tower was completed and the State House bell (now called the Liberty Bell), ordered in 1751, was hung.

The Assembly also ordered a "large Clock to strike on the Bell." Subsequently, its works were installed in the attic of the State House. The clock faces in the end gables were incorporated into structures resembling the head and cases of a tall case clock, the hands being moved by long rods driven by the works in the center of the attic. The steeple bell, however, was not used to strike the hours. A second bell was ordered by the Assembly, in 1752, for that purpose and was placed in a cupola on the main roof just before the tower.

In February 1752, in order to accommodate its committees, the Assembly ordered the erection of a suitable room adjoining the southeast corner of the building. Work was begun immediately, and the room was

Andrew Hamilton, an eminent lawyer and Speaker of the Assembly, superintended the building of the State House. From a portrait copied by Adolf Wertmuller (1751-1811) from an original now lost. Courtesy Historical Society of Pennsylvania.

completed some time during the following year. Demolished around 1812, the chamber was described by a contemporary as "a very elegant apartment." This room also served as the library of the Assembly and was well equipped with sets of English statutes along with works on history and literature.

With the completion of the committee room and library, no additional structures were erected in the State House Yard during the Colonial period. However, other buildings were contemplated. On February 20, 1736, the Assembly reserved the lots on Chestnut Street at the corners of Fifth and Sixth Streets for the erection of a city hall and county courthouse within the next 20 years, but these buildings were not constructed until several years after the Revolution.

The State House and Independence

Philadelphia, the metropolis of English America, was destined to become even more prominent during the American Revolution. As opposition to England's colonial policy developed in America, the city's location near the center of colonial America naturally made it the focal point of government. The long tension between the American colonies and the mother country, which had led to occasional acts of violence in the past,

Two Centuries of Independence Hall

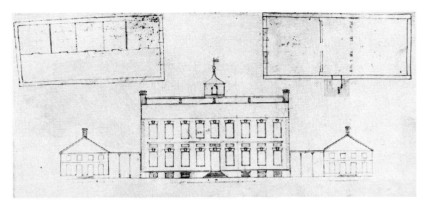

Proposed plan of the State House, 1732, attributed to Andrew Hamilton. The elevation of the main building shows it substantially as first built. A skimpy plan like this seems inadequate to people of the 20th century, accustomed to meticulous architectural drawings. Detailed drafts had not been introduced in the 1700's; rather, the master builders in the field were a combination of what we would call today architects, engineers, and workmen. On them lay the burden of supplying the technical details between the simple sketch and the finished structure. Such a man was Edmund Woolley, master carpenter of the State House. Courtesy Historical Society of Pennsylvania.

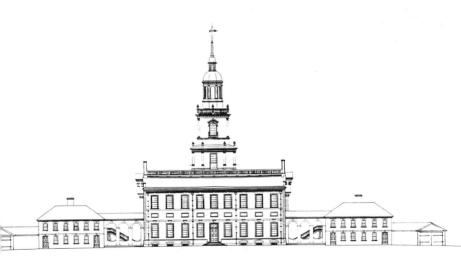

The State House, about 1776, with wing buildings adjoined by wooden sheds. These were used during the Revolutionary War to store ammunition and, perhaps, to shelter Indian delegations at various times. The wings were used as office space and, in part, even as living quarters for the doorkeeper and his family.

11

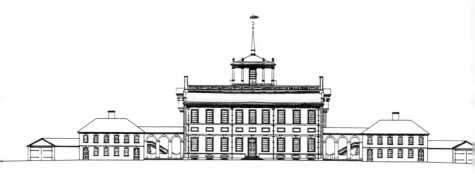

By 1773, the steeple had rotted to a dangerous extent. It had become so weak that ringing of the bell was avoided for fear of toppling the steeple. Though the Pennsylvania Assembly had long intended to remove this badly decayed structure, it was not done till 1781 — the year of the British surrender at Yorktown, Va. After the steeple was removed, the brick tower was covered with a hipped roof, shown here, and the bell hung just below it.

The wooden sheds were removed some time after 1787 to make way for the City Hall on the east (left) and County Courthouse on the west (right). Begun in 1790 and in 1787 and completed in 1791 and 1789, respectively, these buildings fulfilled the original plan of a city governmental center as conceived by Andrew Hamilton. With the establishment of the temporary Federal capital in Philadelphia, from 1790 to 1800, City Hall became the seat of the U.S. Supreme Court and the County Courthouse became Congress Hall.

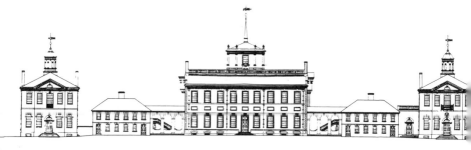

In 1812, the Pennsylvania Legislature permitted the City and County of Philadelphia, which occupied the State House after the Federal and State capitals moved from Philadelphia, to pull down the east and west wings and erect in their places "modern" office buildings, designed by the architect Robert Mills. These buildings were used for the purposes of municipal administration and storing records. Because of the burden on public funds, the State House was dangerously close to being torn down at this time. It was spared that fate when the City bought the group of buildings and the square from the Commonwealth of Pennsylvania in 1818 for $70,000.

Lafayette's visit, in 1824, started a move to lift the State House from neglect and direct attention to it as a shrine. In line with this new attitude, attempts were made to restore the building to its original appearance. The first important step in this direction was the restoration of a steeple to the building. William Strickland, the famous American architect, designed a new one which was constructed in 1828; it was not an exact replica, but followed the general design of its predecessor removed in 1781. The principal deviations were the installation of a clock in the steeple and the use of more ornamentation.

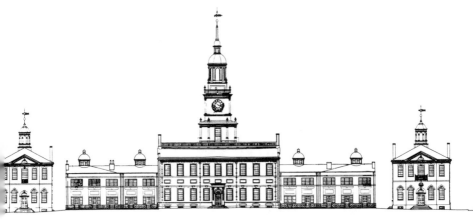

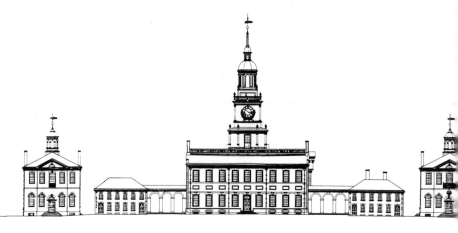

Although various alterations were made to the interior of the State House — by now, generally called Independence Hall — in the mid-nineteenth century, appreciable exterior changes, were not made till just before 1900. Between 1896 and 1898, as part of the City's general program for the restoration of Independence Square to its appearance during the Revolution, the Mills buildings were replaced by wings and arcades which resembled those of the 18th century. The buildings have retained this appearance to the present day.

again erupted in 1773 when a group of Bostonians destroyed a shipment of tea. Instead of making an effort to discover the nature of the Americans' opposition, the English Government attempted to punish them by closing the port of Boston.

The Americans promptly chose representatives to an intercolonial congress which was to become known as the First Continental Congress. This body, composed of leading citizens of the colonies, gathered on September 5, 1774, at the City Tavern before convening formally at Carpenters' Hall, a new building erected by the Carpenters' Company of Philadelphia. Reluctant to adopt a course of open defiance, the Congress sent a petition to the King asking him to restore those rights of Englishmen which Parliament seemed determined to take away. In answer to the English acts of coercion, the Congress turned to economic pressure by calling upon Americans to boycott English goods. Although the First Continental Congress protested strongly against violations of the "rights of Englishmen" claimed for the American colonists, no demand for independence was made.

After the first Congress adjourned on October 26, 1774, relations between the colonies and the mother country grew steadily worse. On April 19, 1775, the Minute Men of Massachusetts fought the British forces at Lexington and Concord, thus challenging the armed might of the British Empire. About a month later, on May 10, the Second Continental Con-

Second Street north from Market showing the early Courthouse in left foreground, one of the meeting places of the Assembly until the completion of the State House. Christ Church is in the background. Engraving by William Birch, 1799. Courtesy Historical Society of Pennsylvania.

gress met in an atmosphere of tension in the Assembly Room of the State House. The governing body, forced by events, moved from protest to resistance. Under the Presidency of John Hancock, the Congress (in June) chose George Washington to be General and Commander in Chief of the Army. The latter, "from his usual modesty, darted into the library-room" when his name was first suggested by John Adams. But after a unanimous election, Washington accepted that commission in the Assembly Room and left shortly thereafter to assume his most difficult duties. Despite the outbreak of warfare, this session of the Continental Congress adjourned on August 1, 1775, without a demand for independence.

When the Congress reconvened on September 1, 1775, in the State House, King George III had already issued a proclamation (August 23, 1775) declaring that "open and avowed rebellion" existed in the colonies. This and other actions of the King, as well as the publication in Philadelphia of Thomas Paine's *Common Sense,* caused public sentiment in favor of independence to grow rapidly in 1776. It was a difficult task, however, to overcome the reluctance of the conservative delegates to make

15

Benjamin Franklin by Benjamin Wilson, 1759. Upon the evacuation of Philadelphia by the British, this portrait was removed from Franklin's house by Captain Andre and carried to England. It was returned to America in 1906 by Earl Grey and is now in the White House, Washington, D.C.

an open break.

Not until June 7, 1776, did Richard Henry Lee, of Virginia, acting on instructions from the Virginia Convention, offer a resolution declaring, "That these United Colonies are, and of right ought to be, free and independent States," and that foreign alliances and a plan of confederation ought to be created. Then, after 2 days of debate, consideration of the resolution was postponed for several weeks. Meanwhile, a committee, composed of Thomas Jefferson, John Adams, Benjamin Franklin, Roger Sherman, and Robert R. Livingston was named to draft a declaration "setting forth the causes which impelled us to this mighty resolution.'' On July 2, 1776, Lee's resolution was adopted after a heated debate in which Adams played a dominant role. Two days later, the Congress formalized this act by adopting the Declaration of Independence. On August 2, after it had been engrossed, the document was signed by most members of Congress. These drastic and irrevocable actions, in effect, marked the end of British authority in the American colonies and the birth of the United States of America.

The Declaration of Independence is one of the greatest statements of the principles of democracy ever penned. Written largely by Thomas Jefferson, it expressed the thoughts and feelings not only of the assembled delegates but also of that part of the American people bent on freedom and independence. These thoughts, expressed in the measured cadence of Jefferson's lines, gave the colonists a creed to be triumphantly established: "That to secure these rights [Life, Liberty and the pursuit of Happiness], Governments are instituted among Men, deriving their just powers from the consent of the governed." Here is the continuing principle now permanently entrenched as the heart of American democracy.

To institute such a government required the agonies of a long, often

Silver inkstand, still preserved in Independence Hall, used during the signing of the Declaration of Independence.

City Tavern, where the delegates to the First Continental Congress gathered, on the morning of September 5, 1774, prior to their formal assembly at nearby Carpenters' Hall. Engraving after William Birch, 1799. Courtesy Philadelphia Free Library.

Carpenters' Hall, built by the Carpenters' Company of Philadelphia, where the First Continental Congress met in 1774.

John Hancock, president of the Second Continental Congress from 1775 to 1777. Copy by Samuel F.B. Morse c.1816 after a painting by J.S. Copley. Independence National Historical Park collection.

indecisive and frequently discouraging war. Throughout the many and hard years of the Revolution, the Congress sat in the State House, except for periods of danger such as the occupation of Philadelphia by the British forces from September 1777 to June 1778. During that winter, Washington's small army endured untold hardships while keeping watch at Valley Forge when the American cause appeared almost hopeless.

In 1778, however, the cause received new strength. Largely through the astute diplomacy of Benjamin Franklin, an alliance was formed with France; and, on August 6, 1778, Conrad Alexandre Gérard, the first French Minister to this Nation, formally presented his credentials to Congress in the Assembly Room.

With the flow of men, money, and supplies from France, the war was brought to a virtual conclusion at Yorktown, Va., in 1781. When Washington's dispatches reporting this victory were received by the Congress in the State House, on October 24, celebrations and general rejoicing were held throughout Philadelphia. About a week later, Congress was presented with 24 stands of colors captured at Yorktown.

The formation of a confederation for the new nation was an even more difficult task than obtaining agreement to the Declaration of Independence, and steps to form such a confederation were taken very early in the Revolution. As a matter of fact, only 8 days after the Declaration was adopted, a draft constitution, called the Articles of Confederation and Perpetual Union, was first reported by a committee to the Congress. In spite of the need for unity to meet the enemy's threat, the States were not willing to commit themselves to the various obligations (small though they now seem) required in the proposed confederation. Maryland, in particular, insisted that, as a condition of her acquiescence, certain other States first surrender their claims to western lands. On July 9, 1778, eight States signed the Articles of Confederation in the Pennsylvania State House. Maryland did not accede until 3 years later, after Virginia, Massachusetts, and Connecticut gave up their claims to the region which became known as the Northwest Territory. However, the new Articles of Confederation, giving the revolutionary government constitutional standing, did not begin their short period of effectiveness until March 1, 1781.

This first frame of government did not attempt to form a powerful national government; under the Articles of Confederation the States retained almost the power of independent nations. However, the Articles did create a Congress which could consider and legislate matters affecting the Nation as a whole. Although they contained certain weaknesses, they held together the 13 States long enough for responsible leaders to discover the kind of government the United States must have.

During those critical years, the State House had served the new nation well as a capitol. As already noted, it was in this building that Congress had organized the national administration and made the necessary plans for carrying the war through to its successful conclusion. The Provincial Assembly of Pennsylvania, meanwhile, having graciously relinquished its accustomed room to Congress, had carried on as best it could in a crowded space on the second floor of the State House.

The occupation of Philadelphia by the British had been a period of distress not only for the American cause but for the State House as well. The building had first been used as quarters for British troops. After the battle of Germantown, it served as a hospital for wounded American soldiers.

These uses of the building had left it, in the words of a member of the Congress, in "a most filthy and sordid situation," with "the inside torn much to pieces." Extensive cleaning and repairs were required to refit the building for meetings of the State Government and the Congress. The Assembly took advantage of this need for repairs to enlarge their temporary quarters in the southeast corner of the upper floor. This was done by removing the partition between their chamber and the "long gallery." The new space then became approximately the same size as the Assembly Room on the first floor.

The Revolutionary period also saw an alteration on the exterior of the State House—the removal of the badly decayed wooden steeple above the brick tower. The Assembly considered this step as early as 1773, but the project was not carried out until 1781. After the steeple was removed, the brick tower was covered with a low, sloping, hipped roof, surmounted by a slender finial.

In 1783, a body of mutinous soldiers surrounded the State House and

Thomas Jefferson, author of the Declaration of Independence. Painting by Charles Willson Peale (c. 1791). Independence National Historical Park collection.

Richard Henry Lee, whose momentous resolution adopted on July 2, 1776, was, in the words of John Adams, "the greatest question...ever...debated in America, and a greater, perhaps, never was nor will be decided among men." Painting by Charles Willson Peale, 1784. Independence National Historical Park collection.

George Washington. Painting by James Peale (c. 1787). Independence National Historical Park collection.

John Adams, one of the most active members of the Continental Congress, and the "ablest advocate and defender" of the Declaration of Independence, played a major role in the achievement of independence. Painting by Charles Willson Peale, before 1795. Independence National Historical Park collection.

demanded back pay. Although the members of Congress were unharmed, the incident led to their moving to Princeton. The Congress of the Confederation never returned to the State House.

"To Form a More Perfect Union"

With the return of peace in 1783 came also postwar depression. Hard times created discontent. By 1786, in Massachusetts, this flared into an open insurrection known as Shays' Rebellion. This affair (perhaps not so serious as often painted) helped point up the weakness of Congress and intensify the movement already begun to amend the Articles of Confederation. A stronger central government was needed. As a result, a convention was called by the Congress.

The Federal Constitutional Convention opened in Philadelphia on May 25, 1787, in the same room in the State House where the Declaration of Independence had been adopted. This room permitted the delegates to meet in secret session, which suggests the seriousness the delegates attached to their responsibilities. The Convention, composed of 55 men chosen by the legislatures of the States, was a small group, but included the best minds in America. As a matter of course, they chose George Washington to be the presiding officer; his endorsement was probably the chief factor in winning acceptance for the Constitution. The leader on the floor, and in some ways the most effective man in the Conven-

State House as it appeared about 1776. Engraving by Trenchard based on detail from painting by Charles Willson Peale as published in the *Columbian Magazine*, c. 1790. Courtesy Philadelphia Free Library.

tion, was James Madison. His efforts were ably seconded by James Wilson, who deserves to be ranked with Madison on the basis of actual influence on the completed Constitution. The aged Benjamin Franklin was the seer of the group; his great service was as peacemaker of the Convention. Gouverneur Morris, brilliant and coherent debater, was responsible for the very apt wording of the Constitution in its final form. Other important delegates included George Mason, Elbridge Gerry, William Patterson, Charles Pinckney, and Roger Sherman.

The purpose of the Convention was, as stated in the Preamble to the Constitution, "to form a more perfect Union" among the States, to ensure peace at home, and to provide for defense against foreign enemies. The delegates believed that these objects could best be achieved by establishing a strong national government, but it was soon apparent that serious disagreements existed as to the nature of this proposed new government. Throughout the hot summer months, the delegates labored. The Constitution was not born at once, but developed gradually through debate, interchange of opinion, and careful consideration of problems. Many minds contributed to its final form. A body of compromises, the Constitution created the central government of a land which is both a nation

"Congress Voting Independence, July 4, 1776." This painting provided much needed evidence for the restoration of the Assembly room. Painting attributed to Edward Savage. Courtesy Historical Society of Pennsylvania.

Christ Church (built in 1727-54) where George Washington, Benjamin Franklin, and other notables worshiped; seven signers of the Declaration of Independence are buried in its grounds and cemetery.

and a confederation of States. It was impossible for the framers to attempt to answer all questions; much was left for future generations to define. As a result, the Constitution has proved to be a most elastic instrument, readily adaptable to meet changing conditions.

On September 17, 1787, 4 months after the Convention has assembled, the finished constitution was signed "By unanimous consent of the States present." The Federal Convention was over. The members "adjourned to the City Tavern, dined together, and took a cordial leave of each other."

Often during the bitterness of debate, the Convention's outcome was in doubt. At the signing, Franklin, pointing to the gilded half-sun on the

Detail photo of rising sun on back of speaker's chair in Assembly room.

back of Washington's chair, observed:

> I have often and often in the course of Session, and the vicissitudes of my hopes and fears as to its issue, looked at that [sun] behind the President without being able to tell whether it was rising or setting: But now at length I have the happiness to know that it is a rising and not a setting Sun.

Completion of work by the Federal Convention was merely the beginning of the struggle for the new Constitution; the crucial part remained. For the framework upon which the Convention had expended so much thought and labor could be made law only by the people. This was to be accomplished by submitting the document to the people for their approval or disapproval in popularly elected State conventions. This method would serve to give the Constitution a broad base of popular support. Such support was particularly necessary, since the Convention made clearly revolutionary decisions in stating that the approbation of 9 States would be sufficient for establishing the Constitution over the States so ratifying, and that the consent of the Congress was not required.

In State after State special elections were held in which the issue was whether the voters favored or did not favor the proposed Constitution. Pennsylvania's State Convention met in the State House on November 21, 1787. Under the influence of Wilson's vigorous arguments, that body ratified the Constitution on December 18. The honor of first ratification, however, went to Delaware. Her convention ratified the document

James Wilson, who, with Madison, had most actual influence on the completion of the Constitution. Artist unknown.

James Madison, sometimes called "the Father of the Constitution." Pastel attributed to James Sharples, Sr., c. 1796-97.

unanimously 11 days earlier. Several of the smaller States adhered shortly thereafter. The sharpest contests took place in Massachusetts, Virginia, and New York where the Anti-Federalists were strong and ably led; but the advantages of the Constitution were so great that it was finally ratified in 1788 by 11 States. Rhode Island and North Carolina held out until after Washington became President.

In order to meet popular objections to the Constitution, the Federalists in Massachusetts drafted amendments which their Commonwealth, in

Robert Morris, financier of the Revolution. Painting by Charles Willson Peale (c. 1782). Independence National Historical Park collection.

Conrad Alexandre Gérard, first French Minister to the United States, who formally presented his credentials to Congress in Independence Hall on August 6, 1778. Painted by Charles Willson Peale, 1779. Independence National Historical Park collection.

"Signing of the Constitution" by Louis S. Glanzman, 1987. Acrylic on canvas, commissioned by PA, DE, & NJ State Societies, Daughters of the American Revolution. Collection of Independence National Historical Park.

ratifying the Constitution, might propose to the other States for adoption. This clever device helped win the struggle in several reluctant States. From these suggested amendments, intended to protect the individual citizen against the central government, the first 10 amendments to the Constitution, called the Bill of Rights, were formed. When the Constitution was finally ratified, the Congress arranged for the first national election and declared the new government would go into operation on March 4, 1789.

The new Federal Government first began its work in New York where Federal Hall Memorial National Historic Site is now located; then, in 1790, the Government came to Philadelphia. The move to Philadelphia resulted from a compromise known as the Residence Act, approved July 16, 1790. This act directed that the permanent capital was to be situated on the Potomac, but it also stipulated that the temporary seat of government was to be in Philadelphia for 10 years. Robert Morris was generally credited with bringing the capital to Philadelphia and was castigated by New Yorkers for his part in its removal from their city.

When the location of the capital was under consideration, the City and County of Philadelphia, as well as the Commonwealth of Pennsylvania, offered the Federal Government the use of the City Hall and the County Courthouse, two new buildings then under construction. These buildings fulfilled the original plan of a governmental center as conceived by Andrew Hamilton. The offer was accepted and for the last 10 years of the 18th century the United States Congress sat in the new County Courthouse (now known as Congress Hall), on the west side of the State House, and the U.S. Supreme Court, in the new City Hall (Supreme Court Building), on the east.

The building in which the Supreme Court sat from 1791 on was erected by the City of Philadelphia to accommodate the growth of municipal departments and functions. During the Colonial period the city government occupied the small courthouse at Second and High (now Market) Streets. When the Federal Government came to Philadelphia, the new building was not yet completed, and the Supreme Court of the United States met first in the Pennsylvania Supreme Court Chamber in the State House. After August 1, 1791, the Supreme Court generally occupied the Mayor's Court, the large room at the south end of the first floor, in the new City Hall. It is possible that the corresponding room on the second floor was also used on occasions by the high tribunal. During its occupancy of the building, the Supreme Court was first presided over by John Jay, who was succeeded in turn as Chief Justice by John Rutledge and Oliver Ellsworth. Here the court began its active work, thereby lay-

This 1799 view shows the Pennsylvania State House without its steeple. It was, from lack of maintenance, torn down in 1781. A new steeple was added in the 1820's. Engraving by William Birch, courtesy Independence National Historical Park.

ing the foundation for the development of the Judicial Branch of the Federal Government.

The ground on which Congress Hall stands was purchased for the Province of Pennsylvania in 1736. Although there had been plans for a long time to erect a courthouse on the lot, it was not until 1785 that the Assembly of Pennsylvania passed an act to appropriate funds for the erection of the building. Work began in 1787 and was completed in 1789. This county court building became the meeting place of the first United States Congress, Third Session, on December 6, 1790. Frederick Augustus Muhlenberg was then Speaker of the House and John Adams, President of the Senate. It is today the oldest building standing in which the Congress of the United States has met.

Before the courthouse could be turned over to the United States Congress, alterations had to be made to fit the building for its new purpose. The first-floor chamber, to be used by the House of Representatives, was furnished with mahogany desks and elbow chairs, carpeting, stoves, and venetian blinds—all of fine workmanship. In addition, a gallery was constructed to hold about 300 people. The Senate Chamber on the second floor was even more elegantly furnished.

Then in 1793, to accommodate the increase in membership of the House from 68 to 106, the building had to be enlarged by an addition of about 26 feet to the back of the original structure. In 1795, a gallery was con-

First Bank of the United States, built in 1795.

Alexander Hamilton, Secretary of the Treasury in Washington's administration, whose comprehensive program placed the new Nation on a firm financial basis. Painting by Charles Willson Peale (c. 1791). Independence National Historical Park collection.

structed for the Senate Chamber as well.

The decade during which Philadelphia served as the capital was a formative period for our new Government. In foreign relations, the Citizen Genèt affair and other repercussions of the French Revolution, which brought near-hostilities with France, ended the historic Franco-American Alliance of 1778. It is impossible to list all the great events which occurred during that period, but among them must be mentioned the inauguration of Washington for his second term in the Senate Chamber on March 4, 1793. At the same time John Adams assumed the Presidency of the Senate. Washington delivered his last formal message before Congress, prior to retiring, in the chamber of the House of Representatives on December 7, 1796. It is this message which some have confused with Washington's famous Farewell Address.

It was in Congress Hall that the first 10 amendments—the Bill of Rights—were formally added to the Constitution. It was here also that the First Bank of the United States and the Mint were established as part of the comprehensive program developed by Alexander Hamilton, Secretary of the Treasury, to rectify the disordered state of Government finances. Here, too, Jay's Treaty with England was debated and ratified; Vermont, Kentucky, and Tennessee were admitted into the Union; and the Alien and Sedition Acts were passed. And it was here that the Federal Government successfully weathered an internal threat to its authority— the Whiskey Insurrection of 1794.

In the chamber of the House of Representatives, John Adams was inaugurated as second President of the United States on March 4, 1797. Two years later, official news of the death of Washington was received here by Congress, at which time John Marshall introduced Henry ("Light-Horse Harry") Lee's famous words: "First in War, First in Peace, First in the Hearts of his Countrymen."

After 1800

With the turn of the century, Philadelphia ceased to be a capital city. In 1800, the Federal Government moved to Washington. During the previous year, the State Government had moved first to Lancaster and later to Harrisburg. Congress Hall and the Supreme Court building reverted to the uses for which they were originally intended—a county courthouse and a city hall. The State House became an empty building, used apparently only at elections.

The Governor, on March 13, 1815, approved an act authorizing the County Commissioners of Philadelphia to take charge of the State House and to rent out the space as they considered advisable. All profits ob-

Congress Hall (looking west along Chestnut Street) near the turn of the century when Philadelphia ceased to be the capital city and the building reverted to use as a county courthouse. In right foreground is old Chestnut Street Theater. Courtesy Independence National Historical Park Collection.

"The Artist in his Museum." In 1802, Charles Willson Peale obtained permission to use the second floor of Independence Hall for his museum. This scene shows the *"long gallery."* Courtesy Pennsylvania Academy of Fine Arts, Philadelphia. Gift of Mrs. Sarah Harrison (The Joseph Harrison, Jr. collection).

tained were to be used to make repairs and improvements on the building.

Having released the State from responsibility for its State House, the Legislature next sought to realize from this property a sum of money to be used in building the new capitol at Harrisburg. In an act, approved March 11, 1816, the Legislature provided for the sale of the square and its buildings. This act required the Governor to appoint three commissioners (none from Philadelphia) to lay out a street, or streets, through the square "in such manner as in their opinion will most conduce to the value of the property." The square was to be divided into lots suitable for building; the total amount to be realized was not to be less than $150,000.

One section of the act, however, saved the State House. This provided that the City of Philadelphia should have the privilege of purchasing the building and square for the sum of $70,000. The City Councils promptly passed an ordinance to purchase the property and took title on March 23, 1818. This was a financial and spiritual investment unequaled in the history of American cities.

Although the City of Philadelphia had saved the State House and its sister buildings from possible destruction, it was evident that many local officials did not consider the ensemble worthy of complete preservation. As early as 7 years prior to purchasing this property from the State, municipal authorities presented the Legislature with petitions requesting that the Commissioners of the City and County of Philadelphia be permitted "to pull down the east and west wings of the state-house...and to erect in their place, suitable buildings for the deposit of the records of said City and county..." On March 24, 1812, this authority was granted by the State Government. The old wings and the committee room were demolished, to be replaced by "modern" office buildings designed by the architect, Robert Mills. These new offices consisted of two row buildings attached to the east and west ends of the State House. Often called "State House row," they were occupied by various officials of the city, county, and federal governments.

Other changes to the State House followed as a result of the City's desire to adapt it for current needs. The Assembly Room, in which the Declaration of Independence had been adopted, was converted into a court room. This was "modernized" by the removal of its paneling and wood trim redecorated in a more up to date style. Furthermore, the Chestnut Street doorway was replaced by a more ornate one with a fanlight to allow more light into the entrance hall.

The first occupant after the State government moved to Lancaster was Charles Willson Peale, who, in 1802, received permission to use the upper floor of the State House (including the tower rooms) and the Assembly Room on the first floor, for his museum which had occupied Philosophical Hall since 1794. By the terms of the agreement, Peale was responsible for the maintenance of both the building and the State House Yard.

In order to make the building more suitable for his museum, Peale removed the alterations made in 1778-79 to accommodate the Assembly, and rebuilt the long room to appear as it did during the Colonial period. The museum, which occupied the second floor of the State House until 1828, included not only an extensive collection of natural history items but also a unique portrait gallery of the great men of this Nation, painted largely by Charles Willson Peale and his son, Rembrandt. Peale also took most seriously his charge to care for the State House Yard, or Garden, as Independence Square was then known. He planted trees, added new gates and benches, and improved the walls and lawns. It was most fortunate that a man of Peale's caliber was responsible for the property's care during this dark period.

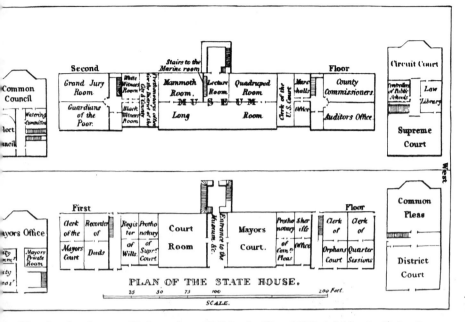

Plan showing the use of Independence Hall by the City of Philadelphia, the Federal Courts and Peale's Museum. From *Philadelphia in 1824.* Courtesy American Philosophical Society.

After Peale's museum moved from the State House in 1827-28, the second floor was rented to the United States Government for judicial purposes. Alterations were made under the direction of the architect, John Haviland, to adapt the space for its new use. The long room was again obliterated, and the western portion of the upper floor was made into one large room for the use of the United States Circuit and District Courts. The partitions in the eastern portion apparently were retained; the northern room became the jury room for the court and the southern room, the office of its clerk. This occupancy of the State House by Federal courts continued until 1854. Consolidation of the city and districts in that year made more room necessary for city offices, and the Federal courts were forced to move. Their place was taken over by City Councils. The court room on the west was occupied by the Common Council. On the east, the partition between the former offices of the court clerks was removed, and a single room was fitted for the Select Council. These Councils occupied the upper floor until 1895.

Independence Square

Until the 1820's, Independence Square was known variously as "State House Yard" or "State House Garden." Originally the land bounded

37

City election at Independence Hall. Elections were held at Independence Hall throughout the Colonial period and for many years thereafter. Engraving by Alexander Lawson after a painting by J.L. Krimmel, c. 1815. Courtesy Historical Society of Pennsylvania.

by Chestnut, Walnut, Fifth, and Sixth Streets had been part of the lands set aside by William Penn as "bonus lots." To each purchaser of a substantial farm or "country lot," Penn also gave a city lot as a bonus. The pieces in this particular square were given to Welsh Quakers who settled in Radnor Township.

By the time the ground along Chestnut Street was acquired to erect the State House, most of the original owners had already sold their parcels. By deed dated October 15, 1730, the first lot on the square was purchased by William Allen for the use of the Province. Within the next 2 years the entire Chestnut Street frontage, extending halfway back to Walnut Street, had been secured. Construction of the State House began in 1732.

The desire to provide a proper setting for the State House was evident from the beginning. In the year that the building was begun, the Assembly considered leveling the site and enclosing it with a board fence "in order that Walks may be laid out, and Trees planted, to render the same more beautiful and commodious." As far as is known, however, the landscaping was not carried out until considerably later.

On February 20, 1736, the Assembly determined on a most important policy. An act vesting the State House and its grounds in trustees provided: "That no part of the said ground lying to the southward of the State House as it is now built be converted into or made use of for erecting any sort of buildings thereon, but that the said ground shall be enclosed and remain a public open green and Walks forever." This provision has been retained as a guiding principle in the development of the square save for occasional deviations. On August 9, 1739, the Assembly ordered "that Materials be prepared for encompassing the Ground with a Wall in the ensuing Spring..." Two years later a shingle roof was added on top of the wall to carry off rain water.

Purchasing the remainder of the square was delayed nearly four decades. On May 14, 1762, the Assembly directed that the balance of the land be obtained, and by 1769 the necessary lots had been acquired. In 1770, the Assembly enclosed the whole square with a brick wall 7 feet high, pierced at the center of the Walnut Street front by a tall gateway with paneled wooden doors, a fanlight and pediment supported on pilasters.

At this time the square contained the State House, with its wings and

Independence Square (State House Garden) in 1800, showing brick wall and high gate at Walnut Street. Engraved by William Birch, 1800. Courtesy Independence National Historical Park.

Independence Square in 1838, as seen from the steeple of Independence Hall. Lithograph by J.C. Wild, 1838. Courtesy Historical Society of Pennsylvania.

wooden sheds, and a small wooden platform erected in 1768. The latter was constructed at the instigation of the American Philosophical Society for observing the transit of Venus across the sun on June 3, 1769. It is believed that the observatory stood south of the State House.

Although landscaping the State House Yard had been long discussed, nothing of consequence appears to have been done in this regard during the Colonial period. At the time of the American Revolution, the square apparently was more or less barren, with no planned landscaping or system of walks. Cannons, which must have been a prominent feature of the yard, were parked within the walls.

With the return of peace, interest was again awakened in improving the grounds. Landscaping was finally begun about 1784 under the direction of Samuel Vaughan, a wealthy Jamaica sugar planter then living in Philadelphia. In addition to the wide central walk of gravel, leading from the tower door to the Walnut Street gate, and the serpentine walks about the perimeter of the square, the most noticeable feature of the yard was the assortment of 100 elm trees presented to the Commonwealth by George Morgan, of Princeton. Shortly after the landscaping was completed, the Reverend Manasseh Cutler visited this square and described it in his journal as a "fine display of rural fancy and elegance."

The trees are yet small, but most judiciously arranged. The artificial mounds of earth, and depressions, and small groves in the squares have a most delightful effect. The numerous walks are well graveled and rolled hard; they are all in a serpentine direction, which heightens the beauty, and affords constant variety. That painful sameness, commonly to be met with in garden-alleys, and other works of this kind, is happily avoided here, for there are no two parts of the Mall that are alike. Hogarth's "Line of Beauty" is here completely verified.

The next alteration of the State House Yard following Vaughan's landscaping was undertaken in 1812. In that year, when the old wing buildings were demolished to be replaced by "modern" office buildings, the high brick walls were removed to allow a "freer circulation of air." In their place was erected in the following year, a low brick wall, about 3 feet high, with a marble coping surmounted by a railing of plain iron palisades. Access to the square was provided by an iron gate on Walnut Street and smaller ones on Fifth and Sixth Streets, about halfway between Chestnut and Walnut.

Other changes affecting the early scene followed in 1876. Along with

Independence Square from Walnut Street, looking north.

41

Triumphal arch for Lafayette's visit to Independence Hall, September 28, 1824.
Engraver unknown, c. 1824. Courtesy Philadelphia Free Library.

such necessary improvements as resodding and new drainage, broad steps were constructed in the center of the Walnut Street front and the corners on Fifth and Sixth Streets. Wide flagstone walks were laid through the grounds in almost every direction from street to street. The later addition of steps on Fifth and Sixth Streets, near Chestnut, substantially established the layout of the square as it is today.

Through the years the square has served varied purposes. It was frequently the scene of mass meetings and public demonstrations. Large gatherings met here in the course of the critical days before and during the early part of the Revolution. The most noteworthy of these occurred on July 8, 1776, when, from the observatory platform—described above—Col. John Nixon read publicly for the first time that document since known as the Declaration of Independence.

Evolution of a Shrine

The "State House" did not become "Independence Hall" till the last half of the 19th century. This change in designation, which began about the time of Lafayette's visit to America, is closely linked with the evolution of the building as a national shrine.

Prior to 1824, there was but little reverence or regard for the State House. The visit of the Marquis de Lafayette to Philadelphia in that year, however, awakened an interest in the building which has persisted to this day.

Elaborate preparations were made for the visit of the celebrated friend of America, much of it centering around the State House, which became the principal point of interest. Across Chestnut Street, in front of the building, was erected a huge arch "constructed of frame work covered with canvas, and painted in perfect imitation of stone." The old Assembly

Room, called for the first time "Hall of Independence," was elaborately redecorated. The walls and ceiling were painted stone color, and windows were "hung with scarlet and blue drapery studded with stars." Portraits of Revolutionary heroes and the Presidents virtually filled the available wall space. Mahogany furniture was "tastefully and appropriately disposed."

Lafayette was formally received in the "Hall of Independence" by the Mayor and other dignitaries on September 28. On the days following, during his week-long visit, the chamber served as his levee room.

The interest in the State House engendered by Lafayette's visit was not permitted to die. In 1828, the City Councils obtained plans and estimates to rebuild the wooden steeple which had been removed in 1781. After heated discussions, William Strickland's design for the new steeple was accepted, a large bell to be cast by John Wilbank was ordered, and Isaiah Lukens was commissioned to construct a clock for the steeple. Work was completed on the project during the summer of 1828.

Strickland's steeple was not an exact replica of the original, but it may be considered a restoration since it followed the general design of its predeccessor. The principal deviations were the installation of the four garlanded clock faces in the steeple.

Within 2 years after rebuilding the steeple, interest was aroused in the restoration of the Assembly Room, or "Hall of Independence." On December 9, 1830, the subject of the restoration of this room "to its ancient Form" was considered by the Councils. Shortly afterward, John Haviland, architect, was employed to carry out the restoration. Haviland reported that "from the best information I can obtain of its former style of finish, it appears to have been similar to the Mayor's Court Room" (i.e., the Supreme Court Room across the hall).

The proper use of the room was always a knotty problem. Following the Haviland restoration, the room was rented on occasions for exhibiting paintings and sculpture. Its principal use, however, was as a levee room for distinguished visitors, including Henry Clay, Louis Kossuth, and other famous personages, in addition to many Presidents of the United States from Jackson to Lincoln.

In the 1850's, and during the critical years of the Civil War, veneration for the State House became even more evident. In 1852, the Councils resolved to celebrate July 4 annually "in the said State House, known as Independence Hall..." This is the first clear-cut use of the term "Independence Hall" to designate the entire building.

Perhaps the best expression of this veneration is in the grandiloquent words of the famed orator Edward Everett, who, on July 4, 1858, said of the State House, or as it has now come to be known, Independence Hall: "Let the rain of heaven distill gently on its roof and the storms of winter beat softly on its door. As each successive generation of those who have benefitted by the great Declaration made within it shall make their pilgrimage to that shrine, may they not think it unseemly to call its walls Salvation and its gates Praise.''

On July 4, 1852, the delegates from 10 of the Thirteen Original States met in Independence Hall to consider a plan to erect in the square one or more monuments to commemorate the Declaration of Independence. For various reasons, their deliberations proved fruitless.

During the years after the restoration of the Assembly Room in 1831, a few paintings and other objects were purchased by, or presented to, the City for exhibition. One of the first acquisitions was the carved wood statue of George Washington, by William Rush, which long occupied the east end of the room. It was not until 1854, however, that the City made any real effort to establish a historical collection for Independence Hall. In that year, at the sale of Charles Willson Peale's gallery, the City purchased more than 100 oil portraits of Colonial, Revolutionary, and early Republican personages.

Following the acquisition of Peale's portraits, the Assembly Room was refurnished with these paintings hung on the walls. On February 22, 1855, the Mayor opened the room to the public. From that day on, many relics and curios were accepted by the City for display in this chamber.

Independence Hall group in the winter of 1840. (Note restored steeple and clock, also doorway on Sixth Street side of Congress Hall.) Lithograph by J.T. Bowen after drawing by J.C. Wild, 1840. Courtesy Philadelphia Free Library.

Earliest known photograph of Independence Hall, taken in 1850 by W. and F. Langenheim. From their "Views in North America" series. Courtesy Philadelphia Free Library.

During the Civil War, the "Hall" (or Assembly Room) served a solemn purpose. From 1861 on, the bodies of many Philadelphia soldiers killed in the war, and, in 1865, the body of President Lincoln lay in state there. Such use of the room was not new, however, for John Quincy Adams, in 1848, Henry Clay, in 1852, and the Arctic explorer, Elisha Kent Kane, in 1857, lay in state in the venerable room.

In 1860, a movement was begun by the children of the public schools of Philadelphia to erect a monument to Washington. When the fund was nearly raised, the Councils provided a space on the pavement directly in front of the Chestnut Street entrance. The statue, executed by J.A. Bailey, was unveiled on July 5, 1869.

According to an act of the General Assembly approved August 5, 1870, the other buildings on the State House Square were to be demolished. Fortunately, this act was never carried out. Instead, with the approach of the Centennial of the Independence of the United States, a committee for the restoration of Independence Hall was named in 1872 by the Mayor. The committee entered upon its duties with energy. Furniture believed to have been in the Assembly Room in 1776 was gathered from the State Capitol at Harrisburg and from private sources. Portraits of the "founding fathers" were hung in the room. The president's dais was rebuilt

45

Independence Hall group in 1853. Engraving of a drawing by Devereux. Courtesy Philadelphia Free Library.

in the east end of the room, and pillars, thought to have supported the ceiling, were erected. The red paint which had been applied to the exterior of the building was removed from the Chestnut Street side. When accumulated layers of paint were removed from the first floor interior walls, the long-hidden beauty of carved ornamentation was again revealed.

During the Centennial restoration project, a large bell (weighing 13,000 pounds) and a new clock were given to the City by Henry Seybert for the steeple of Independence Hall. This clock and bell are still in use.

With the close of the Centennial celebration, Independence Hall experienced a period of quiet, disturbed only by the increasing numbers of visitors. Then toward the close of the 19th century, another restoraton cycle began, but its emphasis was quite different from that of any in the past. Except for the replacement of the steeple in 1828, all restoration work heretofore had been concentrated in the east or Assembly Room on the first floor. Finally, in the 1890's interest extended from the

In 1855, the Assembly Room became a portrait gallery, following acquisition by the City of Charles Willson Peale's oil paintings of Colonial and Revolutionary figures. (Note Liberty Bell on ornate pedestal in corner and Rush's wooden statue of Washington in center background.) Lithograph by Max Rosenthal, 1858. Independence National Historical Park collection.

Assembly Room to the remainder of the building. An ordinance of the Common and Select Councils, approved by the Mayor on December 26, 1895, called for the restoration of Independence Square to its appearance during the Revolution. A committee of City officers concerned with public buildings and an advisory committee of leading citizens were named by the Mayor to carry out the work. On March 19, 1896, a resolution of the Councils granted permission to the Philadelphia Chapter of the Daughters of the American Revolution to proceed with the restoration of the old Council chamber on the second floor of Independence Hall.

Between 1896 and 1898, the committees and the Daughters of the American Revolution carried out a most extensive program of restoration. The office buildings designed by Robert Mills were replaced by wings and arcades which were more like those of the 18th century. The first-floor rooms of Independence Hall were restored, and the Daughters of the American Revolution attempted to restore the entire second floor to its Colonial appearance by reconstruction of the long room, the vestibule, and the two side rooms. A start was made in reconstructing the tall case clock on the west gable, but the clock head was never com-

The body of Elisha Kent Kane, Arctic explorer, lying in state in the Assembly Room of Independence Hall, 1857. Courtesy Philadelphia Free Library.

pleted. Well intentioned as these Independence Hall restorations were their architectural details were designed in the Colonial Revival style rather than researched reconstructions of their 18th century appearance.

With the 20th century, emphasis shifted from Independence Hall to the remainder of the group. Although some restoration work had been done in Congress Hall by the Colonial Dames of America in 1896, their efforts were confined to the Senate chamber and to one of the committee rooms on the upper floor. Additional restoration of Congress Hall was not undertaken until the American Institute of Architects became interested in the matter. In 1900, the Philadelphia Chapter of this organization made a study of the documentary and physical evidence available on the building and began an active campaign for its restoration. Finally, in 1912, funds became available and the City authorized the beginning of work under the auspices of the Philadelphia Chapter. This was completed in the following year, and President Wilson formally rededicated the building. In 1934, additional work was done in the House of Representatives chamber.

The restoration of Congress Hall at Sixth Street brought into sharp contrast the condition of the Supreme Court building (Old City Hall) at Fifth Street. For many years the American Institute of Architects and other interested groups urged the City to complete restoration of the entire Independence Hall group by working on the Supreme Court building. This phase of the program, delayed by World War I, was not completed until 1922.

With the completion of restoration projects, the buildings on Independence Square presented a harmonious group of structures in substantially the appearance of their years of greatest glory. The neighborhood in which they were situated, however, had degenerated into a most unsightly area. Therefore, the improvement of the environs of Independence Hall, containing a large concentration of significant buildings, was the next logical development.

This movement to preserve the historic buildings in Old Philadelphia, and incidentally to provide a more appropriate setting for them, had long been considered. During World War II, the nationwide movement for the conservation of cultural resources became particularly active in Philadelphia, and much was done to coordinate the work of different groups. In 1942, a group of interested persons, including representatives of more than 50 civic and patriotic organizations, met in the Hall of the American Philosophical Society and organized the "Independence Hall Association." This association was the spearhead of a vigorous campaign which resulted in stimulating official action to bring about the establishment of Independence National Historical Park.

Although concerned primarily with the preservation of Independence Hall and the creation of an appropriate setting for the country's foremost historic site, the Independence Hall Association viewed the creation of a historical park as a means of reclaiming some of the neighborhood around Independence Square and preserving many significant historic buildings in the area. This ambitious undertaking required the support and concerted efforts of the City of Philadelphia, the Commonwealth of Pennsylvania, and the United States of America.

Lithograph of Independence Hall in 1876. (Note Bailey's statue of Washington opposite Chestnut Street entrance.) Courtesy Philadelphia Free Library.

Restored Assembly Room of Independence Hall, c.1876. (Note President's dais at far end of room, tile floor, and pillars—then thought to have supported the ceiling.) Courtesy Independence National Historical Park collection.

The Association attained its first victory in 1943 when the Secretary of the Interior designated the buildings on Independence Square as Independence Hall National Historic Site. Although the City continued to operate these buildings, a cooperative agreement between the City and the Federal government ensured their preservation.

The Commonwealth of Pennsylvania became involved in the project at the end of World War II when it authorized the expenditure of funds to acquire the three city blocks north of Independence Square. This began a decade-long program of land acquisition, demolition, and landscaping which transformed a congested run-down area into a dignified approach to Independence Hall.

With the creation of Independence Mall assured, the Independence Hall Association turned its attention toward persuading Congress to authorize a national historical park in Philadelphia. On June 28, 1948 the Association's efforts were rewarded. On that day Congress passed Public Law 80-795 which established the Independence National Historical Park Project"...for the purpose of preserving for the benefit of the American people as a national historical park certain historical structures and properties of outstanding national significance located in Philadelphia and associated with the American Revolution and the founding and growth of the United States…''Within the bounds of the park were the historic sites contained in the three blocks east of Independence Square and several outlying areas including Christ Church and the site of Benjamin Franklin's home.

Soon after this law was passed the National Park Service formed partnerships for preservation with a number of organizations owning sites within the park, such as the Carpenters' Company and the congregation of Christ Church. In the case of the Independence Hall group of buildings, an agreement was signed wherein the City retained the title to the buildings while the Park Service agreed to operate and maintain them.

Even after the park was authorized, it took many years and millions of dollars to make it a reality. Demolition, landscaping, research, restora-

The Assembly Room as restored by the National Park Service. NPS photo by Thomas L. Davies.

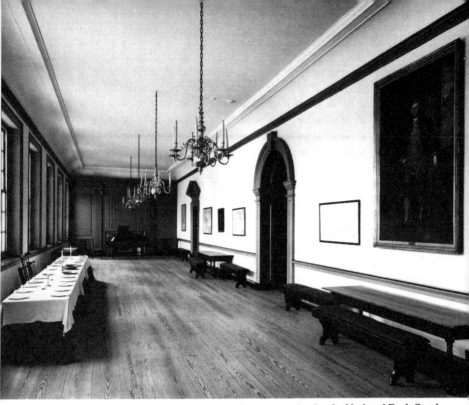

The long gallery of Independence Hall after restoration by the National Park Service.

tion, and reconstruction took place as money could be obtained from both the government and private sources. Finally, the approach of the Bicentennial of the American Revolution provided the impetus to complete the park. Today, the park contains over forty buildings including restored and reconstructed homes and public buildings, museums, a modern Visitor Center, an operating tavern, and even a new home for the Liberty Bell, all surrounded by carefully landscaped grounds. At the physical and spiritual focal point of the park stands the place where it all began, Independence Hall.

As the primary historic structure within the park, Independence Hall underwent an exhaustive twenty year structural stabilization and restoration program. Combing through the enormous amount of documentary evidence and closely examining layers of physical evidence within the building, a team of restoration historians, architects, archeologists and museum curators painstakingly assembled the information necessary to restore the hall to its most historic period. Analyzing paint layers, examining craftsmens' accounts, investigating period building techniques, studying 18th century drawings and engravings of the rooms and scrutinizing evidence remaining of past ''restorations'' helped to identify the great

Governor's Council Chamber after restoration by the National Park Service.

amount of surviving original building fabric, and to unravel the complicated structural history of the building. As a result of this dedicated effort by a team of professionals, visitors today experience the setting of our nation's founding much as the participants themselves did.

The Story of a Symbol

The Liberty Bell is the most venerated symbol of patriotism in the United States; its fame as an emblem of liberty is worldwide. In the affections of the American people today it overshadows even Independence Hall, although veneration for the latter began much earlier. Its history, a combination of facts and folklore, has firmly established the Liberty Bell as the tangible image of political freedom. To understand this unique position of the bell, one must go beyond authenticated history (for the bell is rarely mentioned in early records) and study the folklore which has grown up.

The known facts about the Liberty Bell can be quickly told. Properly, the story starts on November 1, 1751, when the superintendents of the State House of the Province of Pennsylvania (now Independence Hall) ordered a "bell of about two thousand pounds weight" for use in that building. They stipulated that the bell should have cast around its crown the Old Testament quotation, "Proclaim liberty throughout all the land, unto all the inhabitants thereof."

Thomas Lester's foundry at Whitechapel, in London, cast the bell. Soon after its arrival in Philadelphia, in August 1752, the brand new bell was cracked "by a stroke of the clapper without any other violence as it was hung up to try the sound." At this juncture, those now famous "two ingenious workmen of Philadelphia," Pass and Stow, undertook to recast the cracked bell. After at least one recorded failure to produce an instrument of pleasing tone, their efforts were successful, and, in 1753, the bell began its period of service, summoning the legislators to the Assembly and opening the courts of justice in the State House.

With the threat of British occupation of Philadelphia in 1777, the State House bell and other bells were hastily moved from the City to prevent their falling into British hands. Taken to Allentown, the bell remained hidden under the floor of the Zion Reformed Church for almost a year. In the summer of 1778, upon the withdrawal of the British, it was returned to Philadelphia.

By 1781, the State House steeple had become so dangerously weakened that it was removed and the bell lowered into the brick tower. Some 50 years later, in 1828, when the wooden steeple was rebuilt, a new and larger bell was acquired. The old bell, almost forgotten, probably remained in the tower. Years later, many stories arose about how the old bell cracked. Each cited different circumstances and a different date. We do know that in 1846, an attempt was made to restore the bell's tone by drilling the crack so as to separate the sides of the fracture. This attempt failed. The bell rang for the last time on Washington's birthday in 1846.

Now that the bell was mute, useless as a summoner or sounder of alarms, it began to assume a new and more vital role. Over the years it came to be a symbol of human liberty—a very substantial symbol of 2,080 pounds of cast metal—inscribed with the Biblical admonition to "proclaim liberty."

It is difficult to find the exact beginnings of this veneration for the Liberty Bell. Independence Hall, the building with which it is so intimately associated, began its evolution as a patriotic shrine about the time of Lafayette's visit in 1824, but the bell, rarely mentioned earlier, still received no notice.

Probably the first use of the bell as a symbolic device dates from 1839. In that year, some unknown person apparently noted the forgotten inscription on the bell. This was immediately seized upon by adherents of the antislavery movement who published a pamphlet, entitled *The Liberty Bell*. This is also the first known use of that name. Previously,

Speaker's desk in Assembly Room with Syng inkstand and "Rising Sun" chair.

the bell was called the Old State House Bell, the Bell of the Revolution, or Old Independence. That publication was followed by others which displayed the bell, greatly idealized, as a frontispiece. Thus the bell became identified with early antislavery propaganda, invoking the inscription of a promise of freedom to "all the inhabitants." During this time, it is interesting to note, the symbolism of the bell served a narrow field; little, if any, thought was given it as a patriotic relic.

But patriotism was the next logical step. In the first half of the 19th century the bell became the subject of legendary tales which it has not been possible to verify. These legends have been recited in prose and poetry; they have found their way into children's textbooks; and they have contributed greatly to rousing the patriotic enthusiasm of succeeding generations of Americans. Accepted by all classes of people, these legends have done more than anything else to make the bell an object of veneration.

The patriotic folklore apparently began with George Lippard, a popular novelist of Philadelphia. It was Lippard who wrote that most thrilling and irrepressible tale of the bell, the vivid story of the old bellringer waiting to ring the bell on July 4, 1776. This tale first appeared in 1847 in the Philadelphia *Saturday Courier* under the name, "Fourth of July,

An early use of the Liberty Bell as a symbolic device. From R.H. Smith, *Philadelphia As It Is*, 1852.

"The Bellman informed of the passage of the Declaration of Independence." Lippard's legend of the Liberty Bell was incorporated by Joel Tyler Headley in his Life of George Washington, *which ran serially in* Graham's Magazine *in 1854. This illustration appeared in the June issue.*

Between 1854 and 1876, the Liberty Bell stood on display in the Assembly Room on a 13-sided pedestal representing the Thirteen Original States. Sketch by Theo. R. Davis in *Harper's Weekly,* July 10, 1869.

1776,'' one of a collection called *Legends of the Revolution.*

The popularity of Lippard's legend soon brought imitations. The noted Benson J. Lossing, gathering material for his popular *Field Book of the Revolution,* visited Philadelphia in 1848 and recorded the story. This gave the legend historical credence in the minds of Lossing's host of readers. Taking the story presumably from Lossing, Joel Tyler Headley, another well-known historian, included it with certain variations of his own in his *Life of George Washington,* which was published first serially in 1854 in *Graham's Magazine* and then in book form.

Firmly established as history by Lossing and Headley, Lippard's story also found poetic expression. The date of the first poem on this theme has not been established, but, once written, it found its way into school readers and into collections of patriotic verse. The most widely read was probably G.S. Hillard's *Franklin Fifth Reader,* issued in 1871, although the poem had been in popular use for some time before. Beginning with ''There was a tumult in the city, in the quaint old Quaker town,'' the poem became a popular recitation piece which every schoolboy knew. The best known lines read:

> Hushed the people's swelling murmur,
> Whilst the boy cries joyously;
> ''Ring!'' he's shouting, ''ring, grandfather,
> Ring! Oh, ring for Liberty!''
> Quickly at the given signal
> The old bellman lifts his hand.
> Forth he sends the good news, making
> Iron music through the land.

From 1876 to 1885, the bell hung in the tower room from a chain of 13 links. Wood engraving in David Scattergood, *Hand Book of the State House*, Philadelphia, 1890.

The growing legend of the Liberty Bell aroused curiosity in the relic itself, hidden from view in the tower. It was consequently brought down to the first floor of Independence Hall. In 1852, the bell was placed in the Assembly Room—the east room. Two years later the temporary platform holding the bell was replaced by a massive pedestal having 13 sides ornamented by Roman fasces, liberty caps, and festooned flags. By 1856 the bell was topped by an eagle presented by Charles Willson Peale.

The Liberty Bell remained in the Assembly Room until a more intense interest, awakened by the approaching celebration of the Centennial Anniversary, caused it to be moved to the hallway. Here, it was enclosed by a plain iron railing and hung from its old wooden yoke and frame which had been found in the tower.

Visitors in 1876 found the bell displayed in the west room, and by 1877 it was moved again, this time suspended from the ceiling of the tower room by a chain of 13 links. Probably because the inscription was difficult to read while the bell was suspended from the chain, it was lowered in 1884, placed in a large, glass-enclosed oak case, and again put in the Assembly Room. Four years later, the glass case was remov-

The Liberty Bell in a glass case, 1895-1915. From Victor Rosewater, *The Liberty Bell Its History and Significance*, D. Appleton and Co., New York, 1926. Courtesy Appleton-Century-Croft Inc.

ed and a special wheeled foundation was built to allow the bell to be quickly removed from the building in an emergency. Displayed at this time in the tower room, visitors were allowed to touch the bell.

Prior to the First World War, the bell was again encased, until it was finally decided that the bell should remain accessible to the many who wished to touch it. The case was removed, and in 1920 a new base and truck for the bell was designed to ensure its safety.

The growing importance of the Liberty Bell as a patriotic symbol led to requests that it travel to World Fairs and Expositions around the country. More people wanted to see it. The first long journey was in the winter of 1885 to New Orleans and through the South. Later trips took the bell to Chicago in 1893, to Atlanta in 1895, to Charleston, South Carolina in 1902, to Boston in 1903, and to San Francisco in 1915. On each trip the arrival of the bell was the occasion for celebrations by patriotic groups and citizens, many of whom traveled long distances to see and touch the venerated relic. During these trips, however, the crack in the bell increased, and finally its condition became so dangerous that all future long distance travel had to be prohibited.

Displayed in Independence Hall, the Bell attracted thousands of visitors

Installing east wall paneling in the restoration of the Assembly Room. The carpenters are raising a panel unit which was joined and assembled as the original was.

Architectural investigation in Independence Hall, 1956. Above: Removal of paint and restoration of woodwork. Below: Detail of hand-carved decoration after paint removal.

daily. In the early 1970's, the National Park Service began to question whether or not the millions of visitors expected during the Bicentennial of the American Revolution would be able to even see the Liberty Bell. Placed inside the tower room, between the only staircase to the second floor and the main exit of the building, space was limited and the resulting crowding could also damage the original 1750's woodwork of the stairhall.

Delivery of plate girder installed above the Supreme Court Room during restoration of Independence Hall.

It was determined that the bell should be moved. A special pavilion was constructed in 1975 just one block from Independence Hall. In the first minute of the Bicentennial year, the Liberty Bell was placed in its new home. Constructed of glass, this building was designed not to detract from but to focus attention on the bell. Its plain, unadorned hall leads visitors to the bell and clear walls allow a view of the bell even at night. In the distance stands Independence Hall, reminding those who visit of the original home of the Liberty Bell.

From all over the world, people come to see, touch and experience the Liberty Bell. It has served to arouse the patriotic instincts of Americans, and is today surrounded by a cloak of veneration. Even more, it has come to be regarded by countless millions throughout the world as a great symbol of freedom, liberty and justice.

The more secure Liberty Bell Interpretive Center opened in the fall of 2003.

Liberty Bell as displayed in its pavillion across the street from Independence Hall.

Suggested Readings

Bowen, Catherine Drinker. *Miracle at Philadelphia: The Story of the Constitutional Convention*. Little, Brown & Co., Boston. 1966.

Ferris, Robert G. and James H. Charleton. *The Signers of the Constitution*. Interpretive Publications, Inc., Arlington, VA. 1986.

Ferris, Robert G. (Ed.). *The Signers of the Declaration*. U.S. Dept. of the Interior, National Park Service, Washington, DC. Revised Edition 1975.

Greiff, Constance M. *Independence: The Creation of a National Park*. University of Pennsylvania Press, Philadelphia. 1987.

_____. *Historic Philadelphia: From the Founding until the Early Nineteenth Century*. American Philosophical Society, Philadelphia. 1953.

Kimball, David. *Venerable Relic: The Story of the Liberty Bell*. Eastern National, Philadelphia. 1989, (revised 2003).

Milley, John C. (Ed.). *Treasures of Independence: Independence National Historical Park and Its Collections*. Mayflower Books, New York. 1980.

Peterson, Charles E. (Ed.). *Building Early America: Contributions Toward the History of a Great Industry, The Carpenter's Company of the City and County of Philadelphia*. Chilton Book Company, Radnor, PA. 1976.

Sellers, Charles Coleman. *Mr. Peale's Museum: Charles Willson Peale & the First Popular Museum of Natural Science*. W.W. Norton & Co., New York. 1980.